BOOM BABY MOON

By Sean Kelly

Illustrated by Ron Hauge

A Dell Trade Paperback

A March Tenth Book

A DELL TRADE PAPERBACK

Published by
Dell Publishing
a division of
Bantam Doubleday Dell Publishing Group, Inc.
1540 Broadway
New York, New York 10036

The trademark Dell® is registered in the U.S. Patent and Trademark Office.

ISBN: 0-440-50573-9

Printed in the United States of America

Published simultaneously in Canada

November 1993

10 9 8 7 6 5 4 3 2 1

BOOM BABY MOON

In the night-lit room
There was a Kermit-phone
And a Steiff raccoon
And a hardcover copy of
Goodnight Moon
And tape cassettes

And a quilt and sets

Of blocks that teach the alphabet

And a silent dehumidifier
And a space-age
plastic pacifier

And a model of an iguanodon

And a Swiss au pair with a Walkman on

Goodnight fireproof feeding bib

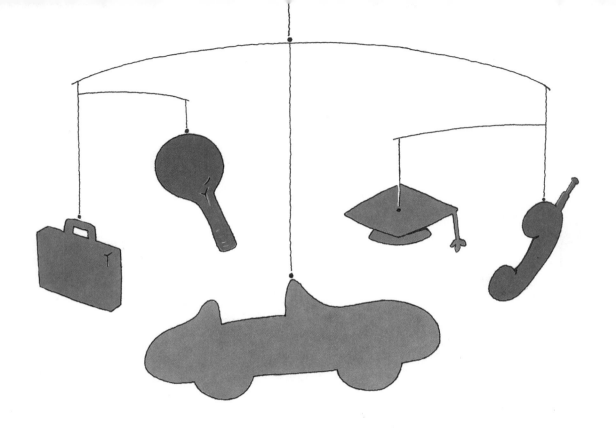

Goodnight mobile of abstract shapes

Goodnight dozens of Raffi tapes

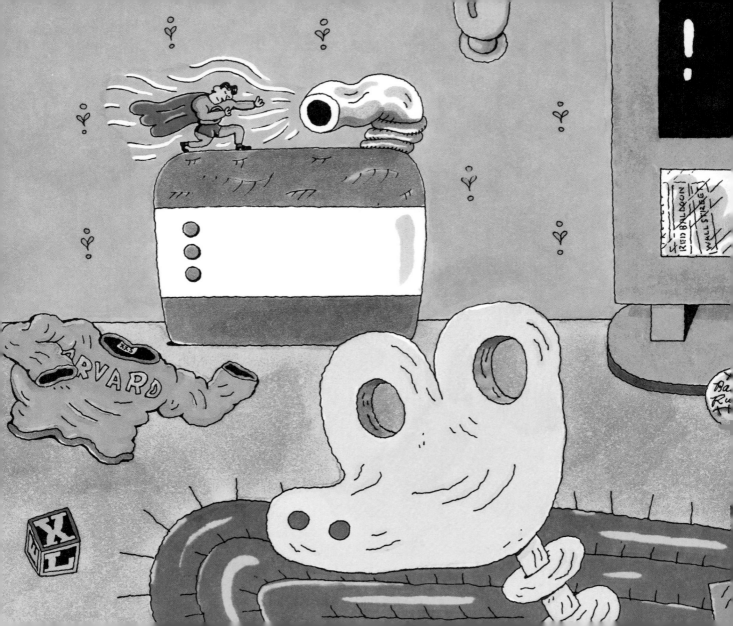

Goodnight Nintendo

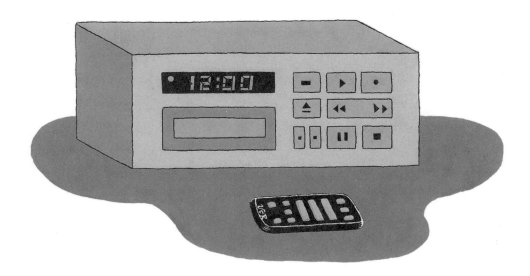

And VCR

THIS IS TO CERTIFY THAT

Dylan

Dr. M.W. Brown

Goodnight certificates of vaccinations

Goodnight play school applications

Goodnight machine that
makes white noise

And motor skill-improving toys

Goodnight contour-cornered, neat
Hypoallergenic sheet

Goodnight orthodontic spoon

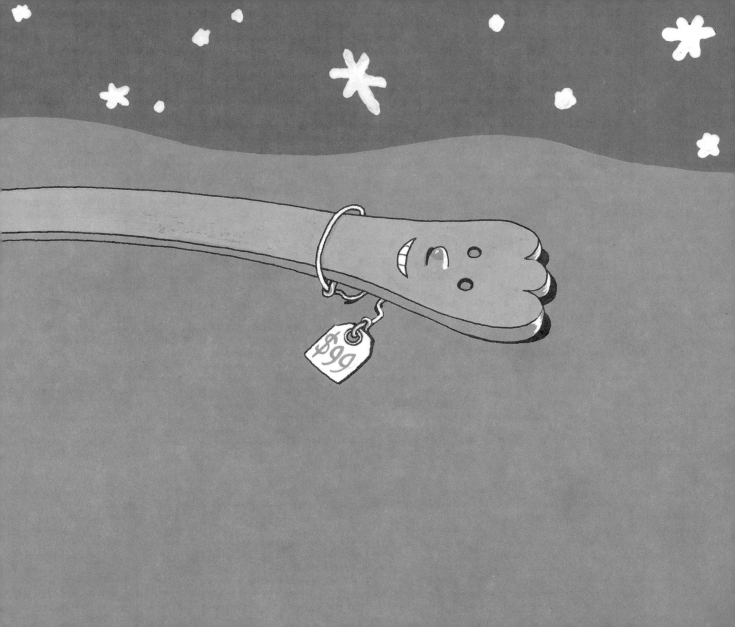

And hardcover copy of

Goodnight Moon